Dear Bride: You're not Alone

7 Steps to Every Brides Perfect Day

Written by: Cemone L Glinton

Follow: Out of Box Weddings @outofboxweddings_

www.outofboxweddings.com

Praise:

Rosalind Roker,

Monique Lightbourne -Coats and Farrah Joseph

Sonia and Aldo Depina

Dana Lynn Photography

Kelly - Sinuchi

Thank you!

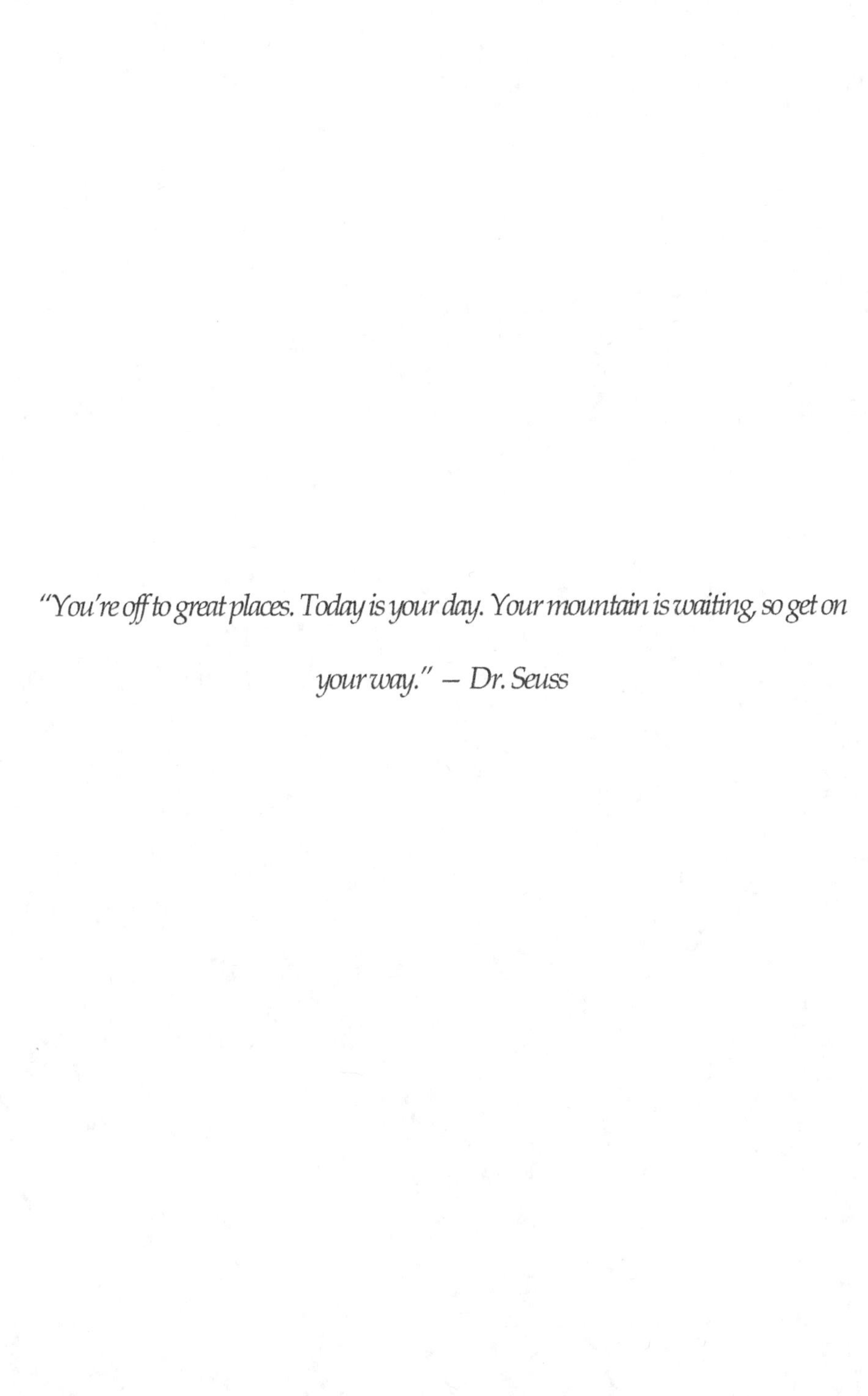

"You're off to great places. Today is your day. Your mountain is waiting, so get on your way." – Dr. Seuss

Table of Contents

Planning a wedding is a process, so be patient, breathe and enjoy.

Dear Bride: You're not Alone

7 Steps to Every Brides Perfect Day

<u>Part I – **IMPORTANT DETAILS COME FIRST:**</u>

In the End It's A Process and You Must Trust It

Towards the end of the planning process, Teri began to get a little nervous. Really and truly, Teri was running low on cash. There were beautiful dinner glassware with silver rims that she wanted to add to her invoice's However, we had already confirmed all her flatware and glassware months in advance. Nevertheless, she greatly desired the dinner glassware with the silver rims. Initially, it was difficult to find a vendor through whom we could rent them. When we did locate a vendor, we gave Teri the cost; it was over a thousand dollars for wine glasses; it was beyond her budget.

From the beginning Teri had made purchases for other items on her own and without the Wedding Coordinator's knowledge. As her Wedding Coordinator, I advised her against the wine glass purchase among other things, but like before and in this case her desire for the wine glassware was stronger than my wisdom.   She wanted what she wanted. There were times she listened and acknowledged my expert advice however, most times she did not.   Ultimately, the wine glassware she really wanted, her budget would not allow, and the reality of it was quite a bit upsetting for Teri.

My Advice or Tip: **Put needs first and wants last**. When your needs come first, this may allow you to have money left in the budget to get some of those details you greatly desire. In Teri's case, she did not adhere to this advice. She later discovered it was too late to make a purchase for something she really wanted.

The Wedding Coordinator tracks costs to help avoid overspending.   Also, the Wedding Coordinator has vendor relationships that can, potentially, save you money as you shop. This means there has to be *integrity* in your communication with your Wedding Coordinator. It is imperative that communication be maintained when it comes to the budget, to avoid similar disappointments or circumstances. Always keep your Wedding Coordinator in your communications.

The wedding planning process should be a memorable and exciting experience. However, so many couples have a feeling of anxiety and worry, especially one or two months prior to their big day. Why is that? Why do couples feel anxious and worried as they get closer to the wedding date? Could it *be perfection*? Wanting everything to be *perfect*? Having absolutely *nothing* go *wrong*? It is practically *impossible* to have anything in life be *perfect*.

My advice or tip: **When it comes to your wedding, it's best to make a plan to follow and follow the plan.**

It's commendable to pursue perfection or to try being a perfectionist; it usually means you place a premium on details, give great attention to details and have specific ideas about *how* you want, *what* you want. As you will discover, with good comes bad. Being a perfectionist has its downfall when planning a wedding. The perfectionist is easily *pegged* a *"bridezilla"*. So, what if you are called a *bridezilla*, it's okay because there's hope even for the *bridezilla*.

So, how do you make sure you're putting your wedding needs first?

Preparation is the key. Pre-planning with your Wedding Coordinator is the best action. Preparation helps avert the fire(s) that can happen on your big day. So what elements are needed in the plan to reduce this potential mayhem? What are the most significant details for you to consider?

Here are some ***must dos***

      1. Hire a Wedding Coordinator

      2. Set your budget

      3. Select date, time, theme, venue, colors

Wait, this is not all of it! What is missing? What other details should you be thinking?

Have no fear, you're not alone and it's quite natural to have these questions.

As your big day gets closer, you want to ensure all goes as close to the plan as possible.

Here are some additional details: Avoid last minute changes, as in Teri's case. She wanted to make a ***major*** change at the last minute. Keep in mind that last minute changes are never a good idea. It can be a meteoric recipe for disaster for you and your wedding team. Yes, there will be small changes; However, changes in important details such as floral, linen and venue should be avoided at all costs.

Set a goal to do very little on the day before your wedding. This should be a time of relaxation. Use this day to relax by the pool with your best friends or take a moment for yourself. Discuss how to accomplish this with your Wedding Coordinator.

Arrange your ceremony rehearsal for the week *before* your wedding. If you have one or two members of the wedding party who are unable to attend, don't worry, proceed with scheduling your rehearsal a week early. Remember, those who may miss the rehearsal can be updated on the wedding day! Of course, the exception to this would be couples planning a destination wedding in another city or country. Remember your goal is to relax the day before.

In the case of rehearsal dinners which can be stressful, have it in advance, but *not* the night before. Take notice that your wedding planning is not a movie, but reality. What does that mean? In the movies it seems as if everything happens quickly almost without a hitch. What the movie doesn't show you is the careful planning and details behind each event that occurs prior to the wedding. As in the case of scheduling your rehearsal, the exception to this suggestion would also be for those who are having a destination wedding.

Make your nail and, if possible, hair appointments in advance and earlier in the week. Try to avoid doing this the day before or make it the *only thing* you have to do the day before. Sometimes it can be awkward for hair appointments, but if at all possible, make them for at least two days in advance. Then on the day of the wedding, have a touch up or finishing touches, but nothing major or time consuming.

Another highly vital factor is the budget. Picture this! Your big day is approaching; time is running out and so is your money. Like in the case of Teri, this is a very common occurrence. However, there is a way to overcome this challenge. The budget section of this book will give you ideas and tips on how to manage and navigate the wedding planning process, with your budget in mind. It's all about discipline – taking care of what's needed first. Later, if your budget allows it, you can add other details or, as I like to say - *"the icing on the cake"*.

Not delegating duties and responsibilities to others is another matter that hinders couples from enjoying the wedding planning process. This task is also for your Wedding Coordinator. It's her/his job to think of and oversee all the details that you may not have considered. I have seen many couples trying to do everything themselves. I have a brides ask me what time I needed them at the venue for set up. Whhatt?? Of course, I thanked them for being thoughtful, but not to even think of it!

On your wedding day, you are to be catered to, pampered and relaxed. You are not to be exhausted because you were setting up the venue hours before you said, *"I Do"*. Most importantly, it is key that you hire someone who is NOT a part of your wedding party. Your Coordinator is not your mom, your sister or your cousin who likes to plan the family's barbecues every year. It is someone who is dedicated to and experienced in making certain your special day is successful.

So, how do you keep calm, cool and collected? What else can you do to enjoy the process and make sure you're getting your needs over your wants?

1. **Be realistic and set a realistic budget.** There are so many wedding ideas from which to choose, but keep in mind that each of them has a cost. Remember the case of Teri and take care of important details first. Hire a Wedding Coordinator. Remember, you want a team that will be there specifically for you and your wedding day. Remember your Coordinator is not a friend or family member. S/he will be able to view your wedding details objectively. S/he will guide you on the *dos* and *don'ts* and those details that are missing or need correction. With this in mind, hiring your Wedding Coordinator means allowing this person to make the tough decisions, especially on the big day. You don't want to know all the gruesome "behind the scenes" details that make your wedding day a success. Sometimes things happen and your Wedding Coordinator won't tell you. Wedding Coordinators make the hard decisions and pray it isn't noticcable. You want a team that is there for your wedding day. You want a team that can make important decisions on your behalf – even in your absence. You do not want anyone who is there for fun or making exciting decisions but avoiding all the complex and intricate ones.

2. **Be consistent with making your vendor payments.** Make monthly payments to venue and all other vendors with balances. You don't want payments due all at

the same time. Set a goal to finish paying all your vendor bills, no later than thirty days prior to your wedding date. Also, know who your vendors are, have clarity about expectations and make certain you are "on the same page". When you have a Coordinator, this is something with which the Coordinator will help and guide you.

3. **Don't be afraid to enlist the help of your wedding party, family, and friends to help you with the small details**. Details such as; seating charts, rehearsal dinners, breakfast for the wedding party, or decisions on who will be ushers. Sometimes couples don't have a chance to enjoy their day because they are trying to take on everything and not delegating duties and responsibilities. Remember having a successful wedding is a team effort. It literally takes a team to make your day a success. I think the most important tip I can give you as you go through your wedding journey is, to understand it's all a process and you must trust it! There will be moments of excitement, fear, anxiety, worry and tears. Well, the tears are usually tears of joy and relief. Your goal is to keep moving forward, regardless of what challenges come.

4. **If you begin to feel overwhelmed, take a break.** More importantly, if you hire a Wedding Coordinator, you will be able to do this. It's alright. You've come a long way and when you're more than fifty percent accomplished, take a few steps back and pat yourself on the shoulder. Take a girls' trip, spend time with your

favorite guy, or do something enjoyable; anything other than wedding planning.

Remember, it's a process! Your team, your Wedding Coordinator, family and

friends will be there to help you through this new and exciting experience.

Welcome and happy planning!

<u>Notes</u>

<u>**PART II – THE GUEST LIST:**</u> A few years ago, I had a client with a total guest list of 100 people. She was determined to stick to it! Well, we began the planning process. About mid-way through, she called to tell me that her mom was feeling a bit hurt and upset. The problem was that her mom was not allowed to invite any of *her* friends to the wedding. These friends included: her mom's best friend, family and neighbors they had known for years. Her mother further explained how some of these people had watched the bride grow up to be the amazing woman she was today. The same was happening with the groom. There was pressure from his parents about who should be invited to the wedding.   I vividly recall this conversation with my clients. When they asked my advice on what to do with guests who were friends of their parents, first I needed to understand their views. This couple wanted to have fun and they were apprehensive about inviting older people to their wedding; they didn't think it would be entertaining.

They were a very social pair; a part of their normal routine was to spend time with close friends eating out, and dancing. As you can imagine, they were somewhat resistant to having older guests at their wedding. Their parents were pursuing them from all directions to reconsider. The bride's mom wanted to know ... How could she **not** invite them? It was almost an insult for them not to be invited. After weeks of pressure, the bride and groom decided to honor their parents' requests. The additional twenty individuals would be added to their guest list. It all came with a cost. Unfortunately, the bride and groom paid for it. The results of this decision caused their guest list to eventually grow out of control along with their budget. When questioned about the dilemma, my reply was that of a concerned Coordinator. I reminded them of our initial conversation - how their budget was important to them and how such a drastic change would affect their overall budget. However, I can sympathize with the parents, it's always a tough decision. As Coordinators, we can only advise, we can't object too much and that's exactly what I did under these circumstances. Was there a way around this? Perhaps there was another way. What I like to recommend to couples is that they have a meeting with close family and friends. The meeting isn't to just get the names for the guest list. The purpose of inviting family and friends is to *discuss* your guest list. Perhaps allowing them to invite three persons and two only is a possible solution! This makes everyone feel included. It also indicates that you want, and value their input during the planning process. During this meeting, you can ask them to give you three to six names of individuals they think should be invited, then put a star next to their top pick(s). Set your disclaimer at the beginning. Make it clear that giving names for the list does not mean they are invited, but that you will need to discuss this with your fiancé. Further, based on your combined lists, you will make your selections. Moreover, inform them that you are on a budget and if they choose to contribute, they are more than welcome. An additional reminder is that it is your wedding and you'll invite whom you choose, unless of course, someone offers to cover the cost of the additional invitees or pay for an expanding guest list. Graciously thank them for their input and move forward. Traditionally, the bride's parents pay for the wedding but, times have changed. More and more couples, together, are funding their wedding with little or no help from the bride or groom's family. As a new couple, this is, in some cases, the first financial decision made together. Starting on *the same page* is essential. **Remember a wedding is for a day, but a marriage is for a lifetime.** Creating a guest list will be one of the biggest challenges in planning your wedding. Think about this - the average person knows about 600 -700 people. Combined, both of you know about 1200 people. So, how do you navigate decisions about who should or should not be invited to the wedding? Here is the *reality*. Yes, it is your wedding and you want to shout it from the mountain top. You have a budget to respect - each person you invite equates to the cost of a meal. Each person invited is another chair purchase; *each person invited increases* your overall budget. Whether you're spending twenty thousand or eighty thousand, there is an amount of money, ideally, you would not like to exceed. That's right! Even my $80,000.00 weddings will have a budget. The average wedding attendee list is between 120 - 200 persons which includes the bride and groom. I understand, you want to invite all the people you know. Your mom wants to invite everyone that has ever known you since birth. However, this is not how it works. You must stay focused on what is important. Remember keeping your guest count under control will greatly impact your overall budget.   Don't ever forget how one part of the budget can affect the other parts *tremendously*. **It's almost textbook!**

Whenever I meet a couple and they tell me their guest list is 100 people, I chuckle inside. It makes me smile because it's not realistic! It takes a highly disciplined couple to create a list of 100 guests out of 1200 people they know and adhere to it- despite all that may come later. More times than not, with a year of planning to go, I have seen that list change from one hundred people to one hundred and fifty people and sometimes even higher. As I mentioned earlier, it takes a lot of discipline to decide on your *guest* and adhere to it. However, applying these tips in this section is sure to give you the *perfect* start.

Consider this: **I strongly suggest you commit to having a RSVP deadline.** Guests who do not RSVP within the timeframe will, unfortunately, not be attending your big day. Of course, there are individuals who will never RSVP, but will show up, for example, your great grandmother or favorite aunt. As your RSVP deadline approaches, sit down one afternoon with a refreshing glass of wine and call those whom you know, more than likely, won't RSVP. Making this effort can minimize surprise guests at the wedding. What if there is an unexpected guest? Well, depending on your catering team, they should be able to accommodate 1 - 2 additional people. However, this is an item to discuss with your catering team far in advance.

Children are another factor to consider when constructing your guest list. Will you invite children? If you're really trying to stay within your budget, consider reducing your children's count or eliminating it. Sometimes this is difficult, and often makes a huge difference. It's always best to make the decision early whether it's feasible to have children attend your wedding. It can be a difficult decision to make especially, if most of your guests are parents of young children. Although, their meals typically cost less, it's still a cost that must be considered. If you know that children will attend your wedding, I recommend you have something special for them, such as coloring books, group babysitting or entertainment. Make arrangements, with your Coordinator, to have a supervised area for them; there they may relax, eat pizza, and/or watch a movie and not cost you $30 for chicken nuggets.

Consider this: I once had a wedding where all the parents *'chipped in'* and paid for a group babysitter. This enabled the parents to really enjoy themselves until the party was over! Both the parents and the children were satisfied.

So, what are some of the questions you should be asking yourself as you develop your guest list?

1.   What is your guest list maximum?

2.   Will single guests be allowed to include a plus one?

3.   Would you like a large or small/intimate wedding?

4.   How many guests will be local? How many guests will be from out-of-town and need hotel accommodations?

5.   Will your parents be allowed to invite guests? If so, how many?

Keep all these questions in mind when you and your spouse-to-be decide who will go on the final guest list. I cannot stress enough how important it is that you ***be inflexible with the guest list plan.*** There will be some exceptions. However, the key is keeping the lines of communication open and stay with the plan no matter what happens.

<u>**PART III - THE BUDGET**</u> I was hired as a full Wedding Coordinator for a lovely couple. They had planned to have their wedding at an estate on the bay; a breathtaking wedding site.   It was going to be beautiful. In the beginning stages of the planning process, we prepared a budget outline based on the venue chosen and the amount of money they wanted to spend. Well, it was almost as if we had not prepared the budget - they purchased details, such as; gold flatware, mirror photo booths, and bartenders the spit fire that exceeded the budget and was against my warnings. More importantly, they had not purchased the most important details such as; catering and photography first. Instead, they were more concerned about the décor and neglected other details that needed their priority attention. Unfortunately, as their wedding day got closer, they were out of money and struggled to make their final payments. When last minute details came up, they had major difficulty. For example, the weather report predicted a great chance of rain.

This meant they would need a tent for the all outdoor venue which was easier said than done. In the end, they were able to add the tent, but it was not factored into their original budget, all though I did factor the tent in the original budget, they would not consider the idea of rain and so the tent plan was dismissed.

The big question most asked when I share this story is… Did they have a budget? Absolutely, and they had a Coordinator! As their Coordinator, there was only so much I could do! Coordinators try to be the *voice of reason*. However, it's not up to us to sign the check and/or make the final decisions.

This is a prime example of a couple who had the right intentions of adhering to a budget but didn't heed the warning.

Keep in mind, your wedding budget is going to be tailored for YOU! After all, it's about YOUR wedding, and YOUR choices. Although it isn't the most enjoyable or the easiest conversation to have, the best decision you can make for your sanity and pockets is sitting down and figuring out your budget's bottom line.

To better understand the importance of having a wedding budget, you must first understand what happens when you do not follow your budget. The rollercoaster of your wedding starts from the moment you answer 'yes' after your significant other pops the big question. Imagine "your wedding"- the moment you've always dreamed is here and you wish to cherish its memory for the rest of your life.   It must be memorably amazing! Before you realize it, you're thrust into making decisions from selecting the dress, the bridal attendants' dresses to the venue and every major and minor detail in between. You begin researching the vendors - photographers, florists, makeup artists, caterers, just to name a few.

Reality! You realize the budget is more than what **you** estimated; Guess what? You can save yourself from this moment of defeat. Creating your budget is not going to take days, you can actually sit down and get it done within an hour or so. When creating a wedding budget, there are just a few decisions that need to be made, which includes the amount to be spent and the priority of the details. All details to be included in the budget are dependent on one another and should be decided at the same time. Details such as; Venue, Wedding Coordinator, Flowers, Decor, Music and Catering.

Creating a wedding budget that fits your requirements, and most importantly, your fantasies - be it an extravagant beach wedding or an intimate event at your place, should be taken into consideration. It is possible to have a realistic budget! Another important factor when creating a budget is *consistency*. You have to visit and update your budget bi –weekly or at minimum once a month. Your wedding details will change as the month(s) progress. It's important to revisit and update your budget so that you're always on track. All it takes is communication and a little planning before the final preparations. So, what other tools would you need to stay within the budget? Staying organized with your wedding budget is extremely important. Having a Planner alleviates most of the stress and anxiety. However, another key ingredient to having a healthy sensible wedding budget is **organization**. What seems to be difficult for most is keeping up with payments and their due dates. Let's face it, if you're planning your wedding one year or more in advance, sometimes it's difficult to remember which payment or deposit you made the previous year. If you're working with a Planner, more than likely, s/he will send you monthly updates of outstanding invoices you may have open with them. What does happen sometimes is that clients make their deposits and then a month before their wedding, they receive a reminder for a final due payment. Can you imagine having five or ten vendors e-mailing you about final payments? In some cases, you may have forgotten about the service(s). I've seen it happen time and time again. Couples get so caught up in leaving deposits, they forget what they've ordered. It happens!

If you are a DIY bride, the important key is to maintain all deposits and payments due in one place, on your calendar, or even better, make an excel spreadsheet. Also, make a habit to pay a little each month on your wedding invoices so when the times comes, and you're thirty days away from your wedding day, you're not feeling the burden and stress associated with payments. Always remember to prioritize your requirements. If you are considering a small intimate reception, invite people who are close to you. Their presence will add meaning to your wedding   versus an "over the top out of control" party that will be sure to cost more than your budget can manage.

Maintain a planner; with a planner it's easy to monitor everything without worrying about missing something important. Enjoy! It's your day! Enjoy and don't let your joy fade amidst all the planning and budgeting. Taking these important details into consideration and putting them into action will help the stress and frustration of DIY wedding planning. Use a personal planner to keep a spreadsheet of vendors and payments. It is a little tedious to track, but once you're committed to keeping track and consistently reviewing your action steps, you will be fine. The importance of keeping a spreadsheet is to show that every month you paid on something. Keep in mind that your goal is to have everything finalized no later than thirty days in advance.

Remember where there is a will - there is a way. There are many resources that are available for you to use to create something rather than ruin your budget with unwise expenses. We love Pinterest, but we've found that many brides go to Pinterest, get their ideas and when they are informed of the cost, they freak out. "OMG! That's too much money or that's way out of my budget, Cemone!".

My strongest suggestion when planning your wedding and using resources, such as Pinterest, is to first, think of the most important details that you need to execute for your wedding day – that is the biggest and most important hurdle. Yes, you want a photo booth and yes, you want carnival dancers, but first things first!   Select a caterer or venue or more importantly decide and finalize your budget. Sometimes a budget can seem like a silly idea, but it's the best idea for a smart and savvy couple.

For our clients with budgets that are 60K, 70K, even 100K, we highly recommend – establishing and maintaining a budget! I'm sure you're thinking - why would a proposed wedding cost of 100k need a budget? Even weddings with an unlimited budget must have financial organization. Otherwise, what would be a 100K wedding plan could spiral into a 300K or 400K wedding cost. Believe me - it's easy to do! Once you start writing the checks, it is easy to overlook or even take notice of the damage you've caused your budget.

Consider this:

I had a wonderful client who had a very limited budget. She wanted to add a giant "love" marquee to her wedding décor, along with a flower wall. We were very early in the process when I advised her to first, let's take care of the most important details. We needed to order linens and chairs and, based on the budget, items such as a flower wall should be left for last. Well… she heeded my advice and waited to make the purchases of the marquee and the flower wall. In the end, she was only able to afford the marquee "love" sign; the wall had to be left out because of her budget. She wanted the flower wall to serve as a backdrop for her bride and groom table. What I promised her was, even though we did not have the flower wall, we would make sure the bride and groom area was beautiful! Needless to say, it was. I will say, even though she took my advice in some areas, it was still difficult for them in others. As we got closer to her wedding day, it was very difficult for her to make her final payments; even to us, as the Coordinators. Can you imagine how much more complicated it would have been had she added a flower wall?

Our personal recommendation is that all payments be finalized, no later than thirty days from the date of the wedding. This client was still making payments up to the day before their wedding. She was a little frustrated with it all. Again, this is a prime example of having and keeping a budget. More importantly, you should prioritize details and listen to your Wedding Planner. Another detail we recommend is to keep the final invoice or quote for each vendor. Do not keep the many preliminary (back and forth) quotes that you may have with the same vendor. What do I mean? We had a client who in the very beginning, when we created her original quote, said it was too much money and she wanted to spend less.   Naturally, I reduced the quote and the services we originally discussed by removing some of the details from the invoice. She was more comfortable and pleased with this pricing and these changes, I thought. Well, a few weeks after the wedding, I received an email with a picture of the original quote. She stated that we did not give her the details that were promised. My first reaction was shock, and then again, I was not, because she completely "flipped the script" on me. I must admit, initially I was taken aback and then it dawned on me. Upon reviewing the e-mail, I realized that she was referencing the original quote and not the quote she finalized. In the end, I had to correct her which is never fun I might add. Typically, brides don't like it when they are wrong, much less told they're wrong by their Wedding Planner. This was an example of someone who had received quote after quote and at some point, she lost track of it.   More than likely, she **had not**

deleted the original quote that exceeded her budget. The **final quote** to which she agreed was not even evidenced in her complaint.

Consider this:

Many times, we see couples argue and fight about their budget. Usually it's the guy telling his fiancée that she is going overboard and he's tired of 'shelling out' the cash. This usually does not end well and the bride is in tears.

Men can be a little more practical than women. In their mind it's just one day and in the end, they must live with the bills. Conversely, women see this as the most important day of their lives and cost cutting is like a dream without an ending or worse, a wonderful dream that she won't remember. Remember, every wedding has a budget; don't be afraid to set your spending boundaries. Long before your wedding day is a distant memory, ask and remind yourself – Do we really want a wedding bill burden? My personal advice…spend wisely!

Because you are a super savvy bride we're recapping and giving you a few tips to remember when it comes to your wedding budget… Enjoy!

- *Communication* is very crucial when it comes to planning your big day. Discuss the plans with your fiancé, family and friends, be clear about your perspective and avoid any future miscommunication. No matter how much you may want to avoid planning discussions, you must, so why not start with an open and honest conversation.

- *Dream* about the wedding you want to have, so you have a better vision about your wedding. It will be an important help to you in the planning.

- *Finances* are the key factor that affect your wedding. Be realistic, sincere and open about your finances. First, figure out who will pay for the wedding, Consider how much they can contribute or is there the possibility of contributions from the immediate families.

- *List your requirements* - the venue, photographers, caterers, dresses - everything you think fits the framework of your ideal wedding. It's a no brainer! Meet with your fiancée, have brainstorming sessions, and write down all your needs and wishes.

- *Research* - If it's your first-time budgeting/planning your wedding without professional assistance, you might have to go out of your comfort zone to search your surroundings. Visit different venues, photographers, dress shops, and caterers. Select the one that provides competitive pricing and quality work, as well.

- *Date selection* - When selecting dates for your wedding, know that selecting public holidays and special occasions may cost more.

For a free budget calculator visit:

http://outofboxweddingcalculator.com/WeddingBudgetCalculator/

<u>**Notes**</u>

<u>**PART IV - HIRING A WEDDING PLANNER:**</u>

One of the first ideas that will come to your mind once you're engaged is hiring a Wedding Planner, What or who is a Wedding Planner? A Wedding Planner helps and guides you through your wedding planning process. Your Wedding Planner becomes your temporary best friend, counselor and advisor. I'd say about 90% of my clients confide and even sometimes cry to me and of course, I'm there to listen. As your Wedding Planner, we have experience and knowledge on the etiquette, and dos' and don'ts of wedding planning. Moreover, an experienced Wedding Planner has made tons of mistakes and more importantly has learned from them. Believe me you don't want a picture-perfect Wedding Planner.   This only means s/he hasn't learned anything and needs to grow more in his/her business. Your Wedding Planner can see the "train wreck" coming at full speed but with their guidance and experience, they will guide you from a total wedding disaster.

Let's face it, planning a wedding only looks glamorous in the movies. For example, Jennifer Lopez in *The Wedding Planner* movie, plays the picture-perfect Planner where the only bad thing that happens is the chicken is well done and the flower girl refuses to drop the rose petals during the ceremony. The best thing that happens is that she falls in love and "rides off into the sunset". I love that movie! It's one of the things that inspired me to start my own business. Is this you? Is this why you've decided to go ahead and plan your own wedding? You probably said to yourself… "I can do that!" "Why am I paying for this – they don't do anything, so I'll take care of it myself". I can't tell you how many weddings we've booked because the bride and groom called us, practically in tears, complaining and practically pulling their hair out screaming, "I can't do this can you help me?" When you're faced with payment deadlines, screaming bridesmaids complaining about how much they hate their dresses, parents wanting to invite every person you've known since kindergarten, music decisions. budget frustrations and what seems like a never-ending list. Guess what? It's at that moment, I promise, you'll regret not hiring a Wedding Planner. Further, if you're fortunate enough, you'll find yourself on the relaxed and blissful list of the elite few who made the best decision for their sanity and hired a professional to help them along the way. Your Planner is there to guide you and offer the best advice possible; most importantly to keep you on track. Clients trying to handle all the details alone have many things to think about. Unfortunately, they get overly involved in details that are important, but not a priority in the "grand scheme" of everything. For example, something that clients get overly involved in is the décor of the wedding. It's a major portion of their budget, usually when it shouldn't be and should not be what the entire day is all about. We **design** weddings as well, so I know how important décor is, but spending six out of the eight months planning and changing décor is unwise and overwhelming. An experienced Wedding Planner prioritizes what needs to be done in regard to your wedding, there is a happy medium to achieve and your Planner can help you stay focused and not go overboard on décor.

Are you convinced yet? Here's another question you may have - "How do I choose a Wedding Planner"? Well that's easy. The best way to choose and select a Wedding Planner is "word of mouth". There are other ways as well, such as -

- Searching online, preferably Instagram, to get an idea of their work – We love IG and it's been the number one location for us to display our talents. If you're not as convinced with IG, try contacting one of the Planners you're considering and scheduling a meet and greet with him/her. Be sure to follow your favorite Planner. Pay attention to their tips and suggestions. Also, be sure to review their blog. What are they talking about? Does it seem as if they have experience or not?

- There are many wedding engines, such as The KNOT or Wedding Wire. These are other excellent resources however, be very careful as they can be misleading and misinterpreted sometimes.

- My very best recommendation is to schedule a meeting and, if possible, observe them in action. Ask them about their next wedding and if you may visit to find out if they *are* the Wedding Planner for you.

- Request a list of previous clients who would be willing to be contacted by you – This will give you direct feedback from the bride about how happy and pleased they were with the Wedding Planner. I would strongly suggest speaking with at least three, if you choose to do this.

Once you've selected at least three prospective Wedding Planners, book your online, over the phone or in person consultations with them. We do not recommend that you choose someone solely by price or because s/he worked well for someone else. We highly recommend that you choose a Planner you feel can do the job; as if it is their personal wedding. Also, consider someone whose personality connects with yours. Remember, your Wedding Planner will become your temporary best friend, counselor and advisor so it's important that you get along with each other.

"You get what you pay for" is the thought that comes to mind.   Having an experienced and knowledgeable Wedding Planner is an investment in your wedding. Why spend hundreds or even thousands of dollars, in some cases, on your wedding only to "go on the cheap" to make it all come to life?

There are several questions you may want to ask the prospective Planner. Here are some, we think are the most important.

- Is my wedding date available?

- How many years have you been in business?

- What has been your most difficult wedding or situation? How did you handle it?

- Talk to me about the day of the wedding?

- How will we communicate? By e-mail, text, or in person?

You may still be asking, "Why should I hire a Wedding Planner?" Well, there are several typical reasons why couples should hire a Planner. Here are a few -

You're just too busy. Let's face it – you would like to do everything yourself, but you can't and although your sister and mother offer to help, they're also busy. Your Event/Wedding Coordinator is there no matter what happens. It is their job to ensure everything is done to the bride and groom's specifications.

Your wedding/event is out of town. For all *destination* wedding brides – having a wedding outside of your town, state or country can be very difficult and stressful. Having a Coordinator representing you at meetings and planning saves time and, in the long run, saves you from potential disappointments. Make sure your Planner is familiar with the destination and knowledgeable about which vendors to contact.

You have a small budget. It may seem that hiring a Coordinator for a small budget may be a silly idea, but it is sometimes the best idea. Your Coordinator will recommend alternatives or other options that can save you time and money. If you cannot afford a Coordinator, hiring the Coordinator the day of your event is helpful and most importantly, less stressful.

You don't **know where to start and are overwhelmed.** Sometimes the idea of flowers, location, makeup, and the reception all seem like a big headache. Hiring a Coordinator is a sure way to organize yourself. It's your Planner's job to do as much as you allow them – take advantage of it!

Have Fun! Give yourself the opportunity to enjoy your engagement – sometimes it can all be overwhelming. Hiring a Planner who is capable is the best way to enjoy your big day and the events leading up to it. Remember this is your moment – the

money you pay for a Planner is worth it!

<u>**PART V – THE WEDDING VENUE:**</u>

Probably the first and most important tasks you'll need to check off your to-do list is finding the perfect wedding venue. Every couple is different and what is perfect for one couple may not be the same for another. Sometimes the perfect venue turns out to be something you've never thought of or perhaps something that you saw online, and it seemed unattractive to you. You went to see it anyway and upon seeing the location, in person, you absolutely fell in love with it.

Consider this: I had a client that was so in love with the idea of a specific venue. She brought the idea to me; it was at the top of her list. Well, we visited the venue and she hated it. She thought it was outdated, smelled weird and absolutely did not like the carpeting. Overall it was not what the pictures reflected when she visited their website. She was looking for a vintage, yet glamorous venue. So, I took her to another venue. This one was modern and glamorous, not vintage, had beautiful chandeliers and no carpeting; she was loved it. This was the venue she finalized and made her deposit.

There are so many venue options from which to choose, it becomes another seemingly, impossible task.   However, once you've accomplished choosing it, it's a huge relief.

When should you decide on your wedding venue? The truth is it's important to do this immediately.   Keep in mind that you're competing with other couples for venues and wedding dates.   Don't get comfortable thinking you can take as much time as you want, and no one is going to book your preferred venue or special date.   Truth is money *talks* and if you're serious about a certain wedding venue for your big day, you should act on it right away and make your deposit almost immediately.

Most venues require a 25% or 50% deposit to hold the date on their calendar. If you're having difficulties with making a large deposit, and you're sure this is the venue you want, inquire about payment arrangements or other options that will give you time and opportunity to make your deposit. Do this without *breaking the bank* to have your prize venue. If you're having difficulties with making the deposit in full, inquire about the following:

1. Can you pay half now and the other half by an arranged deadline date?

2. Can they reserve your wedding date without a deposit and let you know if another couple inquires about it?

3. If you have social media or PR presence, is this an opportunity to barter? Ask the question, you never know.

This is all a part of negotiations, which I'll elaborate later in this section. Granted, there are venues that do not negotiate because they have the clientele and prestige; they have no need to engage in negotiations. However, there are venues that will negotiate in exchange for public relations opportunities or magazine features, if you have that kind of leverage.

Consider this: Our company had a bride that owned a successful public relations agency. The venue was a beautiful and established property. Her company's success gave her leverage, therefore, the venue was willing to negotiate with her on the pricing, as well as give a few perks. Through her PR agency, she offered getting the venue featured in a top wedding magazine. She succeeded in getting the venue featured in the New York Times, Essence magazine and several other major media outlets in print, online, and social media. This was an idea that was very beneficial to the venue and they immediately agreed to it as soon as the bride initially presented it to them. This is a good example of a couple who leveraged what they had to reduce their venue cost and gain extra perks with it!

Here is another experience with one of our favorite couples. We had a bride who was in the selection process for "Say Yes to The Dress", a bridal television program. We initiated negotiations with the venue to be featured on the show, in exchange for the venue to give us a price reduction. Unfortunately, the venue declined. This is a good example of a well-established venue that was not open to an opportunity to barter. Their point of view was that they were uncertain how the show would showcase their wedding venue sufficiently to give a price reduction to our favorite couple. As I mentioned earlier, it doesn't always work but, when it does, it's usually a win/win for all involved parties.

Tips on bartering and negotiating with wedding venues

1. Make sure you have everything in writing, include details such as, with whom you've been communicating, date(s) deals were made, deadlines and any other details you think you may need to reference later.

2. Don't make promises that you know you can't keep. Do not do this – Do not tell them you can get them featured on a major show or that you know David Tutera and can get him to write a blog post about their venue. This is a no, no. You must negotiate with integrity. Be realistic and honest.

3. Make sure all changes are noted on your contract – If you're signing a contract, make sure all signatures that matter are on it - make sure you read the contract and any fine print.

4. Review your details and changes thirty days prior to your wedding with your Planner. Make sure you're covered, and everything is in order.

Sometimes we forget what we promised, especially if time has passed and there are a lot of moving parts to the wedding. As a precaution, be sure to review all the details promised and follow up. If you notice something was not done or is missing communicate it immediately. So, how do you sift through the countless location options and prices? Most couples have an idea of their ideal wedding venue. They're either looking for a church ceremony, garden reception, beach ceremony or ballroom reception. Either way, before you begin looking, have some idea of what your ideal venue looks like. What might I add? Be open to something different as well... more importantly go with your intuition!

When selecting a venue for your ceremony, a church tends to be the initial thought. However, there are some details you must consider. Many churches have rules. Some rules are stricter than others. The restrictions vary from one church to another. Here are some of the restrictions we've personally, encountered.

1. *No rice throwing!* – Typically, most churches would rather you not throw rice, rose petals or anything similar. Most times it's a concern about clean up. If your wedding is on a Saturday, for example, having to clean up rice before services on Sunday can be a bit tedious and impossible. As a result, we're encountering more and more churches that do not allow throwing rice or anything that creates debris on the floor.

2. *No décor other than altar arrangements!* – Especially if the church is already beautiful having décor such as canopies, draping and other details are not necessary. Typically, they want to keep the church as is and no alterations are permitted. Be sure to ask these questions before you pay for anything.

3. *There may be rules about attire!* – Of course, it depends on the church, but women are not allowed to enter the pulpit with their arms exposed. They must wear a shawl. This all depends on the denomination and it is something that must be addressed before you sign their contract.

4. *Do we have to meet with any spiritual leaders?* There may be a rule that requires a meeting with the priest, pastor, overseer, bishop, minister, and so forth. Depending on the religion, you may be required to have marriage counseling or take a certain class before your big day. Please do not assume anything. Make sure you read all documents provided by the church, as well as make sure you're following all the rules that have been outlined for you. These rules apply for destination weddings also.

Consider this: We were contracted for a wedding that would take place in the Dominican Republic. This was a planned destination wedding with a Catholic Church ceremony. Well, amidst all the planning, the couple forgot to do their classes in their home state and have the confirmation sent to the Catholic Church in the DR. Fortunately, we were exactly thirty days away from the wedding date. The bride and groom were able to make an appointment with their priest and complete all requirements before leaving for their destination wedding.

5. The Marriage License Process - Every state and congregation is different. Never assume anything about the marriage license process either. We've planned and coordinated weddings then discovered that the couple forgot to go to the Clerk of the County Court to apply for their marriage license. On the day of the wedding, the minister asked for the license, the bride and groom did not have it; they had not applied for the marriage license! Despite all the plans, all the dreams, and all the hopes, your marriage is not official without a license. You must make sure you have and understand this with whomever is officiating your wedding ceremony; otherwise, you're just having an expensive big party.

6. There are contracts and there's negotiating!   Understand, you simply cannot go to the Ritz Carlton and request a deal at $25.00 per person.   However, if you want the Ritz Carlton and your budget can accommodate the Ritz Carlton, now you're ready for business with the Ritz Carlton or a venue at that level.   If you want to initiate negotiations, focus on the venue that you love and is more agreeable to you. Nevertheless, don't feel disappointed or upset when or if you find a venue that is not interested. The time has come, and you need to make a decision – will you stay with that venue or will you keep looking to find one that is more agreeable?

7. Venue costs are serious! Your venue is one of the costliest purchases you'll incur for your wedding. Your wedding venue is usually about 45% - 55% of your budget. As you're probably beginning to realize, it is the most important. Your venue choice sets the tone and shows much more about your event than you realize. When your guests open their invitation, what might their response be when they see the venue you've chosen? Do you know that the venue is more than just a cost! It is the very essence of your entire event. Why do you think brides change their wedding date for certain venues – it's because they must have it! The venue makes the ultimate statement for your wedding. So, what should you do when you've found the perfect venue and you don't want to say 'yes' to the first offer?

- *First*, ask them to reserve your wedding date, but give you at least a week to discuss the details and come to a final decision.   What does this mean? It reserves the space for you should another couple inquires about the event space. It obligates the venue to follow up with you first before releasing the wedding date you've requested.

- *Second,* request a proposal that includes your estimated number of guests, how much it will cost, taxes, fees and any "add ons". This gives you a more definitive cost and the number of guests you can accommodate. Is this the number you wanted? Can you realistically afford it? Review the proposal very carefully; pay attention to details such as, the type of bar and how many hours, appetizer choices, the number of entrée options, and so forth. Can there be any changes? Can something be reduced? Ask the questions! When conducting business with your venue that includes catering and bar options, an important question to ask is, "How much is my ***minimum spend?***"

What is ***minimum spend?*** Basically, it's the amount of money your event must reach and pay. Be sure to ask if the amount of the *minimum spend* includes *tax and service fees.* When negotiating, make sure you don't overextend yourself – If your cost limit is in the price range of 20K for food and beverage, let the Banquet Manager know you'd like to stay within 15K or 18K just to get their response. You never know, it might work!

If you're getting married in the summer, ask if there are special rates for summer weddings or special rates for military, etc. Counting pennies can help you stay within your budget! Be sure to discuss these details with your intended spouse and your Wedding Planner. In the final analysis, the venue can only do so much. Remember it's important to be prepared and not be disappointed when the pricing is a bit more that what you've anticipated. Further, if the venue has done all they can do and it's not to your satisfaction, just know that you've done your best and it's time to make a decision.

Consider this: We were hired by a couple who came to us with an initial budget of 20K. This amount is on the lower end of wedding budgets, but that's what they thought the going rate for weddings would be in our area; realistically it's not. The average wedding budget in our area is about 30/40k and that's very close and tight.

We went venue shopping.   We viewed and recommended several venues - a total of ten. Some were on the high end and others were on the lower end. She considered all details when it came to select a wedding venue. Well, our bride fell in love with the venue on the high end. We went *back and forth* about it.   We even explained to her how it was going to cost her a lot more once we started to add the details (flowers, draping, staging, etc.). She was insistent and chose the venue that was on the higher end of her budget. The venue itself was 25K excluding any décor. In the end, she chose that venue because she loved it!   We had several possibilities to begin negotiations. For example, the wedding was going to be in the summer and the venue costs were reduced because of it. Additionally, our client was well known in the community which enabled her to promote their business to her network. This created a little more reduction in the pricing. These reductions made the final cost of the venue 21K. This made our client very happy!

Once you've survived negotiations, you're almost there, but not just yet! The contract must be reviewed again. Whatever you have decided about the venue, whether there will be an extended hour of the open bar or extra appetizers, make sure it's all in writing. Give attention to details to assure inclusion of deposit, minimum spend, total amount, menu options, payment options and final payment. Details not included in the contract, should be in writing through e-mail or other official business documentation. Once you've reviewed your contract, proceed to sign and make your deposit. Congratulations! You've survived the first and most important step in planning your wedding—you have a venue. Now the fun begins!

VI – TIMELINE: Once I had a client that insisted on allowing only thirty minutes for their ceremony. Against my better judgement, I went along with it! The reason they wanted a thirty-minute ceremony was because they wanted more time to party at the end of the evening. Well, on the day of their wedding, they were fifteen minutes late, the driver got lost and there was traffic on the way to the venue. They were getting married a five o'clock on a Friday which means there would be lots of traffic. When they finally arrived at the venue, you'll never guess what happened. The groom forgot the marriage license which was in the hotel safe. Can you believe it? At the advisement of the officiant, we decided to go on without the marriage license and start the ceremony. Officially, we were late. We had to shorten the cocktail hour to recover the time lost in the timeline. Did I really have to shorten the cocktail hour? Yes, because it impacted the time set for the dinner service. I had to make sure that dinner was served precisely at the set time.

The Chef was ready to serve and, most importantly, we wanted to make sure guests were served hot, fresh and delicious meals; not food that had been warmed or tasteless. Once we shortened the cocktail hour, everything else was done according to the scheduled time frame.   A few weeks after the wedding. the couple wanted to know why we had not started on time. *I nearly fell off of my chair*, I had to remind them that this is what happens when you allocate thirty minutes for a ceremony without any flex-time for incidentals. As in their case, they had incidentals we couldn't predict. Let's face it – stuff happens. Most couples don't realize the importance of their wedding timeline. The wedding time is the most important part of the wedding; without it there is no wedding. Instead, your wedding becomes a disorganized event on which you've spent hard-earned cash and in the end you're disappointed. How can you have a wedding or event without a timeline?

When planning an event or wedding, it doesn't just happen - the linens don't just appear on the table, the florist does not automatically know to show up, and the guests don't just arrive timely carrying a gift for you. Everything you see, has been precisely planned with great care and thought. Maybe in your mind you may think everything is happening by happenstance. Actually, there's nothing organic about any special event. It's **all intentional.**

Consider this: This one is very personal because it involves one of my best friends. She was having a Spring wedding. Because she chose not to bombard me with any requests or planning on the day of her wedding, I was to be a guest. This was very exciting for me! I'm so accustomed to being behind *the scenes,* it is rare to get dressed up, wear make-up, hair and shoes and be a guest! Rarely do I get to be a guest and celebrate with a few drinks. Throughout the planning process she asked my advice from time to time and I happily gave her tips and suggestions based on my experiences. A few times she mentioned that she was a little displeased with her Wedding Planner, but I encouraged her to give her Planner a chance. I've experienced and know what it's like to have clients displeased for some reason. I thought to myself that maybe my friend was just being dramatic. Anyhow, it was an outdoor estate wedding and the ceremony was scheduled to begin at 5:00 p.m. – I arrived at 4:45. I soon discovered it was a good idea that I had packed my comfortable shoes. Nothing was ready! No, I am not exaggerating! After all, I was the one who told my friend to give the Planner a chance. Nothing was set up and the guests were arriving. It is never good if a wedding is unorganized at the time the guests begin to arrive. I recalled asking my friend, the night before, if she had a timeline and she said."No!" I asked her if she was sure, she said, "Yes". Of course, this was all very strange to me, I mean, how could you not have a timeline? I told her that maybe there was a timeline, but she had not seen it. Well, it turned out that there really was *no timeline.* This meant the wedding day had no schedule or structure. This is not only stressful for the vendors and venue, but also stressful for the Planner – she's flying in the air without a flight plan. As I was about to take my seat, I got a call from one of the bridesmaids. She asked me to take over at the request of the bride. I was more than willing to help. I eagerly went right into action; kicked off my stilettos and very quickly slid into my comfortable flats. That night I ended up directing the ceremony, cocktail hour and reception. The Planner was ill-prepared, overwhelmed and, more importantly, without a timeline. When the Planner was asked about the start time of the ceremony, her reply was "Whenever you (the bride) all are ready". This, of course, was what prompted my friend to use my expertise to rescue her before complete mayhem occurred. In the end, her wedding went beautifully. The night was a success. We worked together to make sure our beautiful bride was happy and, most importantly, she was able to enjoy her night!

The story above is a prime example of the importance of having a precise and detailed timeline. It is important for pre-wedding arrangements and helps the wedding day go smoothly. Keep in mind the order of events depends on the kind of wedding you desire. The details we include in our timeline are as simple as "bride waking up in the morning" all the way to the end when the vendors *breakdown* the room. This may all seem obvious to you, but believe me, having these details on the timeline, make a difference. The timeline details show that everyone is on the same page and know what's expected to take place at any given time. A timeline serves as a guide.

There are several kinds of timelines, such as the wedding planner's personal timeline, vendor booking timeline, photographer's and/or videographer's timeline, caterer's timeline, musicians' timeline, buying wedding dresses timeline, ceremony rehearsal timeline, bridal hair/ makeup timeline, family photos timeline, engagement session timeline and of course, the wedding day timeline.

<u>***Purpose of the Wedding Timeline:***</u> accurately created timeline makes the wedding a seamless experience for the newlyweds and their guests. The timeline must have flexibility in the event something does go wrong, it can be resolved quickly, and there is still maximum time available to get things done before the wedding. What does this mean? Sometimes, we may have clients that insist on having a thirty-minute ceremony time. We, however, recommend allotting one hour for the ceremony. Why? Although the ceremony may only take thirty minutes or less, we still have to consider the time it takes, just in case your transportation is late, someone leaves their written vows in the hotel, a flower girl is crying or even the officiant is late. I've seen it all. Believe me, I highly recommend giving your ceremony one hour. There are benefits to allowing this time. For example, you'll have more time for pictures after the ceremony. There is time just in case the ceremony is delayed, and you can be more relaxed and less stressed because your schedule has built into it - flexibility.

Another purpose for your timeline is the help it gives vendors to complete their work efficiently and reduces the pressure of the workload on the wedding day. It helps the Wedding Planner, bride and groom, the bridal party and the guests keep track of what is happening to follow the organization of the day as much as possible.

Suggestions for Creating the Wedding Timeline:

A well created timeline must prioritize the details such as the bride's wedding day hair and makeup, wedding day preparations and arrival to the ceremony location. The timeline should also indicate details about the reception such as, the first dance, the toasts, the cake cutting and so forth. These details are the important moments to be included and captured by the photographer. As mentioned earlier, it's essential that the photographer, DJ and Wedding Coordinator are on the same page throughout the wedding day. It is very necessary that a schedule for photo sessions are included in the timeline. We highly recommend scheduling a conference call with the photographer at least one week prior to your wedding to review and clarify your expectations, as well as, review your list of most important photos. Further, it's a good idea to review details with your DJ to make sure he has the right songs. It may seem silly, but it makes a difference. The timeline must also include minor details, such as, time of arrival for vendors to setup, playing special songs, names of those giving speeches and making toasts, and announcements by the DJ. In order to properly complete the timeline, we need to effectively communicate with all vendors.

If you're a DIY bride, it's essential that *your day of wedding planner* has all the details about your vendors. For your *day of wedding planner* to complete their job they need accurate e-mail addresses, phone numbers and points of contacts. It's happened to me several times. I was hired as a Day of Coordinator and the clients forgot to tell me that the groom's brother, who was in Afghanistan, was going to skype in during the reception. It was a surprise for the groom and only the DJ and bride knew about it. When putting together the timeline, I had no idea, had we known, we would have made time for it and renamed it a special presentation in the timeline. It was a poignant moment for the couple, but it would have been good for us to know of it and include the special moment in the timeline.

Once the timeline is completed and meets your approval, make and distribute copies of it to the wedding vendors, venue and other people involved in setting up. You need everyone involved to know where they have to be on the day of the wedding and be clear about their roles and responsibilities. We normally send this out no later than one week prior to a wedding. Yes, there may be a few last-minute changes and if there are, we will send out a final timeline the night before. We can't stress how important it is for you (the couple) to take a final look at the timeline prior to going out to your vendors, it shouldn't be taken lightly – the accuracy of the timeline will determine the success of your wedding or special event. As a side note, we love to encourage our clients to provide us with a point of contact other than the bride and groom – someone we can communicate with just in case there are any last-minute changes. It is possible to avoid common mistakes in the wedding timeline by taking a few precautions, such as gathering all the information necessary for the pre-wedding and wedding ceremony and not leaving the timeline for the last minute.

Keep in mind these additional tips when arranging your timeline:

Avoid tight schedules so that there is plenty of time for everything; especially, getting the bride and groom ready, be aware that guests often arrive early so arrange music, drinks and food accordingly and, if there is a Wedding Coordinator involved, especially for the day of, make sure s/he has all the details even the smallest is important to them. Once you've taken these tips into consideration, you're on the right track and ready to create an amazing and well thought out timeline.

VII - ATTITUDE

We planned and coordinated a couple's wedding for over a year.   Towards the end, our relationship with the client was not what we would have liked.   This client was a micro manager and, to be quite honest, a complainer.   They wanted to *point the finger* at something and someone every chance they got it.   I was happy when their day had come and passed.   I breathed a heavy and well needed sigh of relief once I no longer had to do business with them.

For instance, there was a mistake with the linens. Prior to their wedding day, we sent a picture of the table and how it would look with the linens, flowers and place settings to all the vendors, including the company that was delivering the linens. We worked very closely with the company for previous weddings, as well as, this one. The day of the wedding arrived, and the linen company had the wrong linens – when I say wrong, I mean wrong by about four shades lighter. As soon as I saw this, I immediately went into action and informed the linen company that they had delivered the wrong linens and we needed the right ones before the reception start time. Apparently, they used an old invoice and even though they saw the pictures that we sent of the table, the company never questioned the color of the table linens. It was our fault as well because we had not realized before the wedding day that the invoice indicated the wrong linens. There had been so many invoices back and forth between Planner, client and vendor. It was a mess! When the bride and bridesmaids saw the error, they made it a major issue. We assured them that the vendor had returned to their warehouse to bring the correct linens and didn't hesitate to correct the error in time. This wasn't the first time that there was a mistake in the linens, but it was the first time it was my Company's fault. More importantly, I felt terrible about it. It was also the first time the client knew about a pre-wedding issue and was just a few feet away witnessing it all.

Normally when there is problem, as the Planner and the person in charge of the situation, my goal is to resolve the issue. I must admit, we are great at resolving issues. In this situation however, they would not allow my Company to correct the error, instead, they accused us of trying to ruin their wedding. It was a tough moment for me. It is my standard is to work hard for every client. The satisfaction of my clients is my priority; so that moment broke my heart, but I got through it. It made me and the Company stronger and better because of this experience.

Within the hour, we had the correct linens and continued with the day. May I add, this was not the end of issues for this wedding. However, we'll leave that for another book. Despite the issues that occurred, it was the attitude of the couple from the very beginning. We offered to help them find another Planner. We gave them this option because the planning process just didn't seem to be to their satisfaction. Subsequently, we did an amazing job and the wedding went off without any other major issues. In spite of the wedding day being an awesome experience, the client still chose to speak negatively about us. This is a perfect example of taking one moment and amplifying it into something other than what it was in actuality. They not only made negative comments about my Company but also, several of the vendors. This, too, was very sad. We all worked very hard to make their event amazing, but of course it did not matter to them. They did not care that their event was amazing - they just wanted to complain.

Getting married is one of the biggest life-changing events that a person will experience in their lifetime. It's no real surprise that the wedding is also one of the most stressful. There is a great deal of pressure to ensure that the wedding day is perfect. Also, it is an event with so many moving parts, the chances of the day not having any issues are few to none. There will be something that goes wrong. It is how you deal with the miscues that determines just how successful the wedding day will be.

For the bride and groom, maintain a positive attitude and allow those whom you have hired to troubleshoot and manage the day. Allowing them to do their job during the day of and throughout the planning process will mean having a day to remember, no matter how many things don't go exactly as planned. You're probably thinking to yourself what can possibly go wrong? Honestly, there are many things that can go wrong, despite your careful planning.

Saying that you should maintain a positive attitude when planning a wedding is one thing but pulling it off is quite another; it's not as difficult as you might imagine though. There are several things you can do that will help both of you keep a smile on your face throughout the weeks and months it takes to plan your special day. The first thing you need to do is - keep your options open about everything. Many couples have an idea of what their perfect wedding should look like, only to discover that certain elements of their dream wedding are just not manageable. You will be less disappointed, if you do not set your heart on any one thing.

Consider this: There was a time where I welcomed day of Coordinating. Unfortunately, this is a service my Company rarely offers. It was a small and intimate wedding of about fifty people. During the pre – planning process we went through all of the details with the client. I thought I had everything that was needed. About thirty minutes prior to the ceremony, I was approached by the groom with an extra-large sign that the bride specifically wanted hung on a mantel that was the backdrop for the sweetheart table. During the pre -planning, there was no mention of a sign, so it was a quite a surprise when the groom gave the sign to me. I received the sign with specific orders that it must hang on the mantel. Apparently, they were supposed to give the sign to the florist the day before and they neglected to do it. We took the sign to hang on the mantel only to discover that there was no place for it! We tried several methods to get it done - we tried sticking it to the mantel, nails were not allowed to be used on the mantel. We tried calling the florist back, but she had already left. We somehow propped the sign up on the mantel – it could not be hung. I thought it was acceptable considering the circumstances. After all, we were never made aware of the sign until thirty minutes before the ceremony. The wedding began and at the end of the night, the bride thanked us over and over.

A few weeks after the wedding we asked the client for a review. I thought to myself, *the day wasn't perfect, but it was another great event.* There were some last-minute details that surprised us, but we were able to overcome the surprises and get it all done. Was I in for a surprise. She gave us our requested review alright! It was not what we expected. Apparently, she was upset that we did not *hang* the sign and that we did not try. I was shocked! I immediately called her and discovered that she declined to receive any calls from me. Here was another moment where we had worked hard and believed we had done an amazing job, only to find out that the client felt otherwise. More importantly this was an example of a client who chose a negative perception. They amplified a problem that was out of everyone's control and thought to themselves that their wedding was far from spectacular because their sign was propped, not hung. Really?

A good way to stay positive during the wedding planning process is to ensure that it does not become an all-consuming part of your life. It is alright to take a break from the planning every now and then. This is a good way to relieve the stress you are sure to feel. The best way to make sure that you get these little breaks is to start the planning of the big day well in advance. Doing this will also increase your chances of getting everything you want – location, DJ, band, and so forth. Getting what you want will certainly help with having a positive attitude.

Communicate with your wedding coordinator to make sure s/he has everything under control. Still, there will be decisions to make and not every suggestion will meet your approval, but with enough time and patience you and your Planner can work through it without any stress. Always remember there are two ways to deal with wedding stress: you can grumble and complain about what is going wrong and how you wish this and that would happen. You can complain that the Wedding Coordinator or a vendor is not doing his or her job or you can trust the process.

Even with the very best professional help in coordinating a wedding, you are still going to have one or two things not go as planned. The best way to stay positive in these situations is to **_remind yourself_** that you are about to commit the rest of your life to the person you want to be with forever. **_With this thought in mind, let this be reason enough to stay upbeat and positive._**

<u>Notes</u>

<u>Notes</u>

<u>Notes</u>

<u>Notes</u>

<u>Notes</u>

<u>Notes</u>

BIN TRAVERLER FORM

Cut By: _Angheitron_ ✱12 **Qty** 50 **Date** 08/11

Scanned By: ___________ **Qty** _______ **Date** ___________

Scanned Batch ID's

___________________ ___________________ ___________________

Notes / Exceptions

____